For Tricia Johnson, who has rescued
many abandoned dogs and
filled their lives with love
NJS

To Lenny & Benno
RB

Text copyright © 2023 by Nicola Jane Swinney
Illustrations copyright © 2023 by Romy Blümel

First US edition 2024
First published by Big Picture Press, an imprint of Bonnier Books UK, 2023

Library of Congress Catalog Card Number 2024930237
ISBN 978-1-5362-3841-9

24 25 26 27 28 29 TLF 10 9 8 7 6 5 4 3 2 1

Printed in Dongguan, Guangdong, China

This book was typeset in Kitten Days, CentSchbook BT, and Brandon Grotesque.
The illustrations were carved out of acrylic paint on celluloid and colored digitally.

BIG PICTURE PRESS
an imprint of
Candlewick Press
99 Dover Street
Somerville, Massachusetts 02144

www.candlewick.com

101 DOGS

An Illustrated Compendium of Canines

Nicola Jane Swinney

illustrated by Romy Blümel

B P P

Contents

About This Book

There are about 350 breeds of dog in the world, so this book does not cover all of them. Instead, we have picked out some popular breeds along with some more unique ones. So you will find a shar-pei—with its extraordinary folds of skin—next to the sleek greyhound, and the hairless Xoloitzcuintli next to the flufftastic Samoyed.

We should point out that the illustrations of the breeds are not to scale. All measurements have been taken at the shoulder. If different types of a breed exist (e.g., toy, miniature, standard), the range given encompasses all sizes.

If, after reading this book, you would like to welcome a dog into your life, please be sure to do your research and adopt or shop responsibly. Many areas have breed-specific adoption agencies, while others have all kinds of breeds for adoption. If you're unsure, fostering dogs is a great way to introduce yourself to the responsibility of pet ownership while providing a safe environment for a dog in need of a temporary home. Whatever you choose, be sure to consult a veterinarian about providing your pet with safe and responsible healthcare.

From Wolf to Weimaraner

A dog's love is unparalleled. Anyone who has ever owned a dog will know this to be true—your dog will be delighted to see you, whether you've been away for five minutes or five months. Just got up? Can't be bothered to shower? Whatever you do, whatever you look like (or smell like), your dog will be happy with you just as you are.

We don't know when exactly humans first tamed the wolf—the ancestor to all of today's dog breeds—but we do know that our desires shaped those breeds into what we needed. Fisher dogs of the Canada coast, which helped their masters by hauling in nets and leaping into the sea to grab the escaping catch, developed thick, waterproof coats; strong rudder-like tails; and even webbed toes to make their job easier. Sled dogs of the north, which used to pull heavy loads across miles of snow, grew a double-layered coat for extra warmth and were muscular enough to pull heavy loads.

Many of the breeds that have been shaped over centuries no longer do the job for which they were once required. But that doesn't mean all dogs are pampered pets. Dogs are vital to our daily lives, and life without them would be unthinkable: guard dogs, police dogs, sniffer dogs, rescue dogs, service dogs, gundogs, hunting hounds, herders, terriers, and more.

Today's purebred dogs are still in demand, whether an enchanting bichon frisé, a faithful golden retriever, or a glamorous Afghan hound. They come in all shapes and sizes too, from the tiny Chihuahua to the mighty English mastiff, which is the world's biggest dog. Another enormous breed is the Tibetan mastiff, which holds the record for the most expensive dog; one sold for almost two million dollars in 2014. It's a lot of money, but that unconditional love all dogs give? That's priceless.

Groups

Dogs have been bred by people since prehistoric ages, but official classifications as we recognize them today have existed since the late nineteenth century. Dogs have been bred with special characteristics in mind in order to perform certain jobs, such as hunting or herding. Today, kennel clubs and registries work together to create breed standards. The seven main groups are:

Working Group

These strong, intelligent breeds were developed to assist with manual labor—including pulling sleds or carts, guarding, and protecting.

Terrier Group

Feisty, stronghearted, and short-legged, terriers were first bred to go underground to flush out rodents and other small animals.

Sporting Group

This group was bred to track game (both on land and in water) and includes retrievers, pointers, setters, and spaniels. They are known for their companionable traits and good natures.

Toy Group

Bred to be the perfect companions,
and not for working purposes, these
little dogs are attentive and sensitive.

Herding Group

These shepherd dogs were bred to herd
and protect livestock. They are known
for their lively and obedient personalities.

Hound Group

Bred for both exceptional sight and
hearing, hounds are natural explorers
and hunters and are highly independent.

Non-Sporting Group

This diverse group of dogs is tricky
to categorize, but the trait that binds them
together is that they have not been bred
for sporting purposes. Most of these dogs
were bred to help humans.

Doggy Details

All dog breeds share the same basic makeup,
which they inherited from their wolf ancestors.

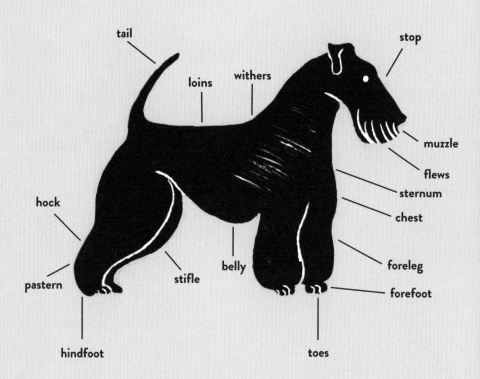

tail

stop

loins

withers

muzzle

flews

sternum

chest

hock

foreleg

pastern

stifle

belly

forefoot

hindfoot

toes

Characteristics

Today, there are an estimated 350 recognized dog breeds, ranging from dapper dachshunds to shaggy sheepdogs. There are a seemingly endless number of physical characteristics that make up the perfect pooch, but listed here are some of the most common ones.

Head

Broadly speaking there are three types of head shape:

dolichocephalic
(long and narrow)

brachycephalic
(short and wide)

mesaticephalic
(medium proportions)

Ears

Dogs' ears are one of their most endearing
and expressive features. There are three
main types and a variety of shapes.

erect

drop

semi-erect

Coats

The range of coat colors, textures, lengths, and patterns is huge and includes hairless, short, long, curly, corded, and fluffy.

hairless

curly

long-haired

Designer Dogs

Our dog breeds have been shaped over the decades by our desires—for shepherding, guarding, hunting, tracking, and retrieving. There are also dogs that are intentionally bred from two different breeds. These crossbreeds have become very popular and are much loved.

Another favorite crossbreed is the Labradoodle—a mix of Labrador and standard poodle. Labradoodles can be more hypoallergenic, making them a desirable choice for people with allergies to canine dander.

Other fashionable crosses include the Maltipoo (a Maltese-poodle cross); cockapoo (a cocker spaniel–poodle cross); sprocker (a springer spaniel–cocker spaniel cross); goldendoodle (a golden retriever–poodle cross); springador (a springer spaniel–Labrador cross); Pomsky (a Pomeranian-husky cross); and puggle (a pug-beagle cross).

Pekingese

This is a little dog with a lot of personality. Pekes (as they're also known) were bred in ancient China for royalty, and they have never forgotten this! Behind those melting brown eyes and long silky hair is a strong, and sometimes stubborn, personality: the Peke likes to get its own way. It is also brave—and doesn't seem to realize how small it is, squaring up to much bigger dogs. But Pekes are jolly little dogs that are affectionate and loyal and ideally suited to apartment living.

....

Life expectancy 12–14 years | **Height** 6–9 in (15–23 cm) | **Trainability** Good, but has a stubborn streak | **Grooming** Lots, due to all that hair | **Exercise** Very little required | **Likely to say** A little pâté would be lovely. | **Unlikely to say** I'd really like a salad.

Basenji

In its native Africa, the basenji is known as "the dog that doesn't bark." While many dogs are often said to be eager to please, that just doesn't apply to this one. It is lively, inquisitive, and playful, but it does have a stubborn streak. The basenji will easily learn what you want to teach it, but whether it will obey your commands depends entirely on its mood. That inquiring mind can be a problem, too, as anything you leave lying around is likely to be investigated by your basenji—usually by means of chewing! All that said, the basenji makes a lovely pet as it adores people and playtime.

....

Life expectancy 13–14 years | **Height** 16–17 in (40–43 cm) | **Trainability** Intelligent, but may not obey! | **Grooming** Little needed | **Exercise** Plenty of stimulation | **Likely to say** I wonder what those shoes would taste like. | **Unlikely to say** Your wish is my command.

Tibetan Mastiff

It may look like a giant teddy bear, but this mighty mastiff is not the dog for everyone. While it has a gentle and loving nature, its sheer size can be a bit off-putting, and it is strong-willed. The Tibetan mastiff sees itself as an equal, rather than a pet, and can be very stubborn. Thousands of years ago, monks known as lamas used these amazing dogs as guards—not many people would confront a dog weighing up to 150 pounds (68 kilograms). Living in high altitudes, the breed developed their thick coat to cope with the harsh climate.

....

Life expectancy 12 years | **Height** At least 24–26 in (61–66 cm) | **Trainability** Clever but stubborn | **Grooming** Needs brushing but doesn't shed much | **Exercise** Regular walks | **Likely to say** I will let no one past. | **Unlikely to say** Can I sit on your lap?

Tibetan Spaniel

This little dog likes to climb! Almost catlike, it will try to find the highest perch from which it can watch over everyone and everything. Thought to resemble a small lion, it was highly prized as a watchdog. This watchful quality has been bred into the Tibetan spaniel for thousands of years, and it takes its role very seriously. But don't expect your dog to be happy on its own. Tibetan spaniels like company and get bored quickly—left to themselves they are likely to bark.

....

Life expectancy 12–15 years | **Height** 10 in (25 cm) | **Trainability** Learns quickly if it wants to | **Grooming** Weekly brushing |
Exercise Short walks | **Likely to say** I bet I can get up there. | **Unlikely to say** No, I'm fine, you can go off and leave me all alone . . .

Afghan Hound

With its slender face, long silky hair, and lithe body, the Afghan hound is surely the supermodel of the dog world. As well as being one of the most beautiful breeds, the Afghan is possibly the oldest. It comes from Afghanistan, where it was known as tazi and was used to hunt dangerous animals, such as leopards. It was not only brave, but also extremely fast, capable of running at speed for many miles. Its independent nature means it does like attention, but on its own terms.

....

Life expectancy 12–18 years | **Height** 25–27 in (64–69 cm) | **Trainability** Independent and can be challenging | **Grooming** Lots of brushing | **Exercise** Needs plenty of room to move | **Likely to say** Look how beautiful I am! | **Unlikely to say** Let's cuddle.

Lhasa Apso

The Lhasa apso was once a watchdog, guarding palaces and monasteries in Asia thousands of years ago. It therefore has a very protective nature. It has been said that when a Lhasa apso looks in the mirror, it sees a lion! But alongside this loyal and watchful nature is an affectionate little dog that loves to play. One of the most delightful things about this breed is that it stays puppyish until it's about three years old. But be warned, the Lhasa apso does like to do its own thing and may not be as easy to train as you'd like. It's not a breed for those who lack patience.

Life expectancy 12–15 years | Height 10–11 in (25–28 cm) | Trainability Has its own opinions | Grooming Lots of brushing | Exercise Plenty of play | Likely to say I need to check that out! | Unlikely to say Of course I will do as you say.

Siberian Husky

It's clear that pet dogs are related to wolves when looking at this handsome breed, which often howls instead of barks! The most striking features of the Siberian husky are its bright blue eyes and "face mask"—markings that frame the eyes and muzzle and change as the breed gets older. Selectively bred by Indigenous people of Siberia called the Chukchi, this breed was trained to pull sleds for long distances across snow. It is therefore obedient, but has a lot of energy. It's well known as being an escape artist if its physical needs are not met, so it needs a well-fenced yard.

Life expectancy 12–14 years | **Height** 20–24 in (51–61 cm) | **Trainability** Smart, but doesn't always want what you want | **Grooming** Regular brushing | **Exercise** Lots! | **Likely to say** What's on the other side of that wall? | **Unlikely to say** I don't want a walk, thanks.

Japanese Chin

In Japan, the chin was bred to have a higher status among dogs and thought to be ideal for noble companionship. Modern chins are one of the most catlike breeds and make charming pets since they are loving and playful. They like to climb and often clean their face with their paws. Looking at their lovely, long fluffy coat, you might think this pretty little creature needs lots of brushing. Not so—the chin is a wash-and-go kind of dog, only needing weekly grooming.

Life expectancy 10–12 years | Height 8–11 in (20–28 cm) | Trainability Intelligent but gets bored easily | Grooming Regular brushing and an occasional ear trim | Exercise Very little | Likely to say Can I sit with you? | Unlikely to say I want to be alone.

Akita

A strong and sturdy dog, the Akita once guarded Japanese royalty. It is fiercely loyal and, for such an imposing breed, very loving. One Akita famously waited for his owner at the train station every day for nine years after he had died. One thing that can be startling is its habit of holding things in its mouth—including your wrist! It isn't going to bite you; it simply wants to take you to where it wants you to go: often to its leash to go for a walk or to its bowl because it wants to eat. The Akita doesn't often bark but it does make a lot of cute noises. Some owners say their dog mutters under its breath!

Life expectancy 10–14 years | **Height** 24–28 in (61–71 cm) | **Trainability** Intelligent but willful | **Grooming** Sheds a lot | **Exercise** Lots of long and interesting walks | **Likely to say** Come and see this! | **Unlikely to say** I'm not at all interested in whatever you're doing.

Shiba Inu

The smallest of six dog breeds native to Japan, the Shiba Inu greets the world with quiet dignity. But it's like a little ninja warrior, moving quickly and nimbly. The Japanese have three words to describe this breed, *kani-i* (spirited boldness), *ryosei* (good nature), and *soboku* (modesty). It also tends to be possessive. Like a moody toddler, the Shiba Inu doesn't like to share, and if it could speak, its first word would be *mine*. It's also a natural hunter, so if you let it off the leash while out on a walk, it will probably disappear in the direction of the nearest squirrel.

Life expectancy 13–16 years | **Height** 13–17 in (33–43 cm) | **Trainability** Has a stubborn streak | **Grooming** Very little | **Exercise** Needs a good daily workout | **Likely to say** Paws off, that's mine! | **Unlikely to say** Of course, I'm happy to share.

Pharaoh Hound

This elegant hound was bred to hunt gazelle more than 4,000 years ago. Despite its storied past, the pharaoh loves people and simply loves life. It's a natural clown—you can even teach a pharaoh to smile! And it's possibly the only breed that can blush—when it's happy or excited, its nose and ears will turn a deeper shade of pink. A hunting hound, it has a strong prey drive and is likely to chase anything it sees, so keep it on the leash at all times.

Life expectancy 12–14 years | **Height** 21–25 in (53–64 cm) | **Trainability** Easy | **Grooming** Very little | **Exercise** At least thirty minutes a day | **Likely to say** Watch this! | **Unlikely to say** I don't want to play, thank you.

Shar-Pei

This extraordinary breed looks like it needs ironing! Those deep wrinkles serve a purpose, though. The shar-pei, whose name translates as "sand skin," is a loyal protector. They were bred as guard dogs since they don't take kindly to strangers. They have also been called "tomb dogs" because statues resembling shar-pei were found in tombs dating back two thousand years. But don't let all that put you off—though it may look like it's permanently frowning at you, the shar-pei is intelligent and makes a loyal and devoted pet.

....

Life expectancy 8–12 years | **Height** 18–20 in (46–51 cm) | **Trainability** Easy | **Grooming** Very little | **Exercise** Adaptable—will enjoy long walks but doesn't mind loafing around | **Likely to say** I will protect you. | **Unlikely to say** (to strangers) Sure, come on in.

Greyhound

This sleek and elegant creature is known as the Ferrari of the dog world. And this is no idle boast; the greyhound can run at speeds of more than 44 miles (70 kilometers) per hour. Greyhounds were treasured by Cleopatra as well as Britain's Elizabeth I. Their love of this breed led to greyhound racing being dubbed the "sport of queens." From that title, you might think the breed needs masses of exercise, but the greyhound is surprisingly laid-back. It is a sprinter, not a long-distance runner, so a daily walk is enough. It will, however, want plenty of belly rubs!

Life expectancy 10–13 years | **Height** 27–30 in (69–76 cm) | **Trainability** Wants to please you. | **Grooming** Very little | **Exercise** A daily walk | **Likely to say** Please rub my belly. | **Unlikely to say** Let's go on an eleven-mile hike!

Saluki

This ancient breed is thought to take its name from the Arabian city of Saluk. Prized for its speed and keen eyesight, this dog chased down hare, fox, and gazelle alongside hunters on horseback. It was also considered a noble companion, and precise records were kept of its breeding. There were once two different types of salukis—desert and mountain—but the two have merged into the modern breed. It has, however, retained its beauty and some of its speed, so be prepared to do a lot of jogging.

Life expectancy 10–17 years | **Height** 23–28 in (58–71 cm) | **Trainability** Intelligent but opinionated | **Grooming** Weekly brushing | **Exercise** Daily runs | **Likely to say** Make sure you get my best side. | **Unlikely to say** It's okay, I'll sleep on the floor.

Alaskan Malamute

This impressive breed is one of the oldest in the world and has changed very little, still resembling its wolf ancestors. It was used by the Mahlemiut people to pull sleds and hunt seals. It is a strong and imposing animal, but it isn't much use as a watchdog—Malamutes regard everyone they meet as friends. They rarely bark, but make a charming "woo-woo" noise. They're intelligent, too, which means they can easily get bored—and a bored Malamute is trouble. They love to dig up the lawn and sniff across kitchen counters for something tasty, so keep them busy!

Life expectancy 10–14 years | **Height** 23–25 in (58–64 cm) | **Trainability** Easy, but can get bored | **Grooming** Needed every day | **Exercise** Lots! An energetic breed | **Likely to say** This looks like a good spot to dig! | **Unlikely to say** (to anyone) You shall not pass!

Shih Tzu

Have you ever seen anything more adorable? Its name means "little lion" but the shih tzu is a lover, not a fighter. Sweet-natured and affectionate, it will happily follow you from room to room. To sum up its personality, it was once described in a magazine as "a dash of lion, several teaspoons of rabbit, a couple of ounces of domestic cat, one part court jester, a dash of ballerina, a pinch of old man, a bit of beggar, a tablespoon of monkey, one part baby seal, and a dash of teddy bear."

....

Life expectancy 10–18 years | **Height** 9–11 in (23–28 cm) | **Trainability** Intelligent but can be tricky to housebreak | **Grooming** A good daily brush | **Exercise** Very little | **Likely to say** I love you! | **Unlikely to say** I am not in the least bit interested in what you're doing.

Chow Chow

This dog may look like a teddy bear, but you'd have to be brave to cuddle a chow chow. It was once a pet for Chinese emperors and has retained its regal bearing. Aside from its impressive coat, the chow chow's unique feature is its blue-black tongue. According to Chinese legend, at the time of the world's creation a chow licked up a few drops of color when the sky was being painted. One of its earlier names was *hei shi-tou*, meaning "black-tongue dog." The chow chow is one of the oldest dog breeds in the world.

....

Life expectancy 8–12 years | **Height** 17–20 in (43–51 cm) | **Trainability** Requires patience | **Grooming** Needs brushing several times a week | **Exercise** Daily walks | **Likely to say** I was royal once. | **Unlikely to say** Let's snuggle.

Xoloitzcuintli

Life expectancy 13–18 years | Height 10–23 in (25–58 cm) | Trainability Loves to learn | Grooming Wipe skin daily with a damp cloth |
Exercise Daily walks on the leash | Likely to say I feel a little naked. | Unlikely to say I've just washed my hair and can't do a thing with it!

Named for the Aztec god Xolotl, the Xoloitzcuintli (*show-low-itz-queent-lee*)—or Xolo (*show-low*) for short—were prized among the Indigenous people in pre-Columbian Mexico and are still highly regarded there today. Xolotl, who was often depicted with a dog's head, was connected to the afterlife, and it was believed that the Xolo could guide human souls to the underworld. This breed comes in two sizes, toy and standard, and is notable for typically being hairless. It may need a coat in colder climates and, depending on conditions, vet-approved sunscreen.

Samoyed

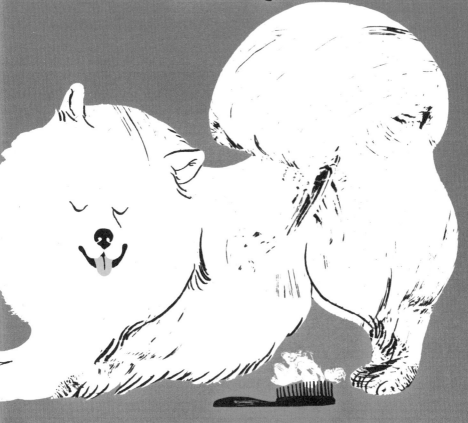

If you're not instantly bowled over by that gorgeous, fluffy coat, then you will certainly fall in love with the famous "Sammy smile"! The Samoyed comes from Siberia, where it was used by nomadic people to hunt, herd, and pull sleds across the snow. It even has ready-made snow shoes—thick hair between the pads—so packed snow doesn't build up on its feet. Its coat, which is usually pure white, has a double layer to keep it warm in the harshest weather. The Samoyed's traveling owners were smart—they slept with their dogs to keep them cozy at night.

Life expectancy 12–14 years | **Height** 19–24 in (48–61 cm) | **Trainability** Needs consistency | **Grooming** Needs daily brushing | **Exercise** Gets bored easily, so needs lots of exercise | **Likely to say** Let's go and play in the snow! | **Unlikely to say** I'm too cold.

Pug

There is something particularly endearing about the pug's squashed face and large, slightly bulging, round eyes. Its origins date back to China, where flat-faced dogs were popular. Bred to be companions, pugs are sweet-tempered and affectionate. Though it is loving, it also has a willful streak that can make training a challenge. But pug devotees say that's part of their charm. The Latin phrase *multum in parvo* (a lot in a little) sums up the pug perfectly.

Life expectancy 13–15 years | **Height** 10–13 in (25–33 cm) | **Trainability** Intelligent but challenging | **Grooming** Occasional brushing | **Exercise** A daily walk | **Likely to say** Come on, let's snuggle on the sofa. | **Unlikely to say** I'll do anything you like.

Great Pyrenees

This beautiful breed takes its name from the Pyrenees mountains, which form a natural border between France and Spain. These dogs have been in the region for thousands of years and were used to guard and herd flocks of sheep and goats. Their ability to access narrow paths through the mountains meant they were also used to smuggle goods, since they could avoid checkpoints. In 1645, King Louis XIV named it the Royal Dog of France. Calm and even-tempered, Great Pyrenees make wonderful pets.

Life expectancy 10–12 years | **Height** 25–32 in (64–81 cm) | **Trainability** Intelligent but independent | **Grooming** Needs regular brushing | **Exercise** Lots—this is an energetic dog. | **Likely to say** Would you like me to round up the children? | **Unlikely to say** No, I don't want to play.

33

Pomeranian

With its foxy little face and fluffy coat, the Pomeranian—known to its devotees as the Pom—is a lively character, with charm and personality in equal parts. The Pom is an extrovert and loves meeting new people. The trouble is, it doesn't know it's a little dog—in its head, it's huge! This can be a problem, because it won't think twice about squaring up to a much bigger dog. But it is undeniably cute, with a pointy muzzle, large eyes that sparkle with intelligence, and a proud stance—see how it trots along with its tail held high over its back.

....

Life expectancy 12–16 years | **Height** 6–7 in (15–18 cm) | **Trainability** Needs lots of patience | **Grooming** Daily brushing | **Exercise** Surprisingly active and it loves daily walks | **Likely to say** (to bigger dogs) Come at me if you're so tough! | **Unlikely to say** I don't like strangers!

English Mastiff

The direct ancestor of this impressive dog was called the Molossus and lived some 5,000 years ago, which means the mastiff is one of our most ancient breeds. Famed for fighting as well as bull- and bear-baiting, the mastiff was also used as a guard dog and hunter. Its name comes from the Latin word *mansuetus*, meaning "tame," and the modern breed, despite its size, is gentle and quiet. The only drawback is drool—and lots of it!

Life expectancy 6–10 years | **Height** At least 27–32 in (69–81 cm) | **Trainability** Responds well to lots of praise | **Grooming** Weekly brushing | **Exercise** Two walks daily | **Likely to say** Can I sit on your lap? | **Unlikely to say** Off you go, I'll be fine.

Chihuahua

The Chihuahua is a feisty, funny, and fun-loving breed from Mexico. There's an awful lot of personality in that tiny body—the Chihuahua is officially the world's smallest dog breed—and it won't let you forget it. It likes to be involved in everything you do and wants to be with you all the time. This is why you often see Chihuahuas being carried around in custom-made bags and baskets. There are two types, smooth-haired and longhaired, both of which make delightful little pets.

Life expectancy 14–16 years | **Height** 5–8 in (13–20 cm) | **Trainability** Easy | **Grooming** Occasional brushing (more for the longhaired variety) | **Exercise** Daily walks | **Likely to say** Where are we going today? | **Unlikely to say** I'm not interested in what you're doing.

Neapolitan Mastiff

Everything about this ancient Italian breed, also known as the mastino, screams power. Its huge, wrinkled head was described as "astounding" by the American Kennel Club. Those velvety face folds hang almost down to its muscular chest, and it moves with lumbering purpose. It takes its name from Naples, where it was developed as a guard dog. As a pet, however, it is loving and gentle, and only wants to sit on your lap—all 190 pounds (90 kilograms) of it—and drool lovingly over you.

....

Life expectancy 7–9 years | **Height** 24–31 in (61–79 cm) | **Trainability** Needs firm training, can be headstrong | **Grooming** Weekly brushing and frequent face wiping | **Exercise** Plenty | **Likely to say** Who goes there? | **Unlikely to say** I'm going to get you!

Maltese

That pure white coat is extremely glamorous, but the Maltese is much more than a cloud of silky hair. Although it's a little dog, it has plenty of personality and is very much a "people person." The Maltese was kept as a companion dog and it loves human company, so much so that it can get quite anxious if separated from its owner. It is intelligent and quick to learn, but can be destructive if bored or left alone. If you want a dog that wants to be with you all the time, pick a Maltese.

....

Life expectancy 12–15 years | **Height** 7–9 in (18–23 cm) | **Trainability** A quick learner | **Grooming** Regular brushing | **Exercise** Play and short walks | **Likely to say** Take me with you! | **Unlikely to say** I don't miss you at all.

Borzoi

The word *borzoi* comes from the Russian word for "swift." This elegant hound was bred in Russia for use in hunting rabbits, foxes, and wolves, usually working in teams. It is a sprinter rather than a distance runner, but its instinct to chase anything—and we mean *anything*—that runs can be a problem if you let it off leash. Its beautiful silky coat doesn't shed much, and it has a naturally sweet manner that makes for a lovely family pet. But despite its hunting heritage, the borzoi is a couch potato.

....

Life expectancy 9–14 years | **Height** At least 26–32 in (66–81 cm) | **Trainability** Easy | **Grooming** Weekly brushing | **Exercise** Less than you might think | **Likely to say** I see a rabbit! | **Unlikely to say** I have no intention whatsoever of chasing that rabbit.

Chinese Crested

Once a Chinese crested dog falls in love with you, it's yours for life. It's thought that these little dogs first came from Africa or South America, but in China it was bred to be a small companion dog. There are two kinds: the hairless, which has silky hair on the head (crest), tail (plume), and feet (socks); and the powderpuff, which has a full coat. Both types can be found in the same litter. Its appearance is rather endearing and it has a charming character, but it's not a good pet if you are going to be out a lot.

Life expectancy 13–18 years | **Height** 11–13 in (28–33 cm) | **Trainability** Can be stubborn | **Grooming** Variable | **Exercise** Very little | **Likely to say** Can I come? | **Unlikely to say** Let's go meet lots of new people.

Keeshond

From the Netherlands, this breed is also known as the Dutch barge dog because it once acted as a guard on boats going up and down the many canals and rivers of this lowland country. Though it will certainly bark to let you know someone is approaching, the keeshond just loves people, so it's unlikely to stop an intruder. You will be able to tell when your keeshond is happy because it will spin in excited circles, working up quite a head of steam! Left to its own devices, though, it can become a nuisance barker.

Life expectancy 12–15 years | **Height** 17–18 in (43–46 cm) | **Trainability** Smart and a quick learner | **Grooming** Twice-weekly brushing | **Exercise** A good walk a day | **Likely to say** Come and say hello! | **Unlikely to say** I will bite you.

Yorkshire Terrier

The Yorkie, as it is affectionately known, is one of the smallest breeds, but also one of the most popular. Its long, silky coat—often set off by a jaunty topknot tied with a bow on its head—is its crowning glory, in rich tan toned with steel gray. It has a feisty personality and, like most terriers, is an efficient ratter—no rodent is safe! But it makes a loving and charming companion, well suited to apartment living, and can be carried around with you wherever you go. Like most terriers, it doesn't like to be left alone or left out.

....

Life expectancy 11–15 years | **Height** 7–8 in (18–20 cm) | **Trainability** Can be tricky | **Grooming** Daily brushing | **Exercise** A walk or play session once a day | **Likely to say** What are we doing today? | **Unlikely to say** Of course I won't chase that squirrel.

English Bulldog

The English bulldog is one of the most instantly recognizable breeds of dog, with a massive head, flat face, bulging eyes, huge chest and shoulders, and narrow hips. Its forehead is wide and it has an undershot jaw, so its bottom teeth are visible when its mouth is closed. It carries itself with dignity, and its sweet temper belies its ferocious appearance. Despite the breed once being used in the practice of bullbaiting, it likes nothing more than to snuggle with you.

Life expectancy 8–10 years | **Height** 14–15 in (36–38 cm) | **Trainability** Can be slow to learn | **Grooming** Occasional brushing | **Exercise** Daily walk to maintain weight | **Likely to say** Can we spend the day in bed? | **Unlikely to say** Do you want a fight?

Cavalier King Charles Spaniel

Cavaliers have the "puppy-dog eyes" expression down to a fine art—it is almost impossible to get angry at them. Kings and queens going back to the sixteenth century have favored these adorable little dogs; one was even said to have been found hiding in the skirts of Mary, Queen of Scots, after she was beheaded. They were especially popular with England's Charles I and his son Charles II, hence the name. Although spaniels were traditionally used to assist on hunting trips, the Cavalier makes a loving and gentle pet.

Life expectancy 12–15 years | **Height** 12–13 in (30–33 cm) | **Trainability** Intelligent and eager to learn | **Grooming** Brushing three or four times a week | **Exercise** Daily walks and lots of play | **Likely to say** I didn't mean to. | **Unlikely to say** I won't do it again.

Canaan Dog

Dogs mentioned in the Bible were the forerunners to the modern Canaan dog. They were used to herd and guard flocks of sheep. When the Romans destroyed Jerusalem in the year 70 CE, and the Israelites were forced to flee, their dogs were abandoned. Those dogs took refuge in the Negev, a rocky desert that spreads across Israel and Palestine, and the descendants of those dogs were redomesticated around 1935, saving the breed that is now the national dog of Israel. The Canaan dog has been used by Israel's military to detect mines and by the Red Cross, but it also makes an attentive pet.

Life expectancy 12–15 years | **Height** 19–24 in (48–61 cm) | **Trainability** Intelligent and engaging | **Grooming** Little brushing | **Exercise** An hour a day | **Likely to say** Let's try something new. | **Unlikely to say** I don't want to.

Papillon

There are two versions of this dainty breed. The papillon has erect ears that look like the open wings of a butterfly—*papillon* is the French word for the insect—while the phalène has folded ears like the wings of a moth, which is what *phalène* means. This little dog was a favorite of French society—Marie Antoinette and Madame de Pompadour both owned papillons. Despite its size, the papillon has a big-dog attitude and will cheerfully boss around anyone—including you—and anything, such as other household pets. It is a lively and alert fizzing little ball of energy.

Life expectancy 14–16 years | **Height** 8–11 in (20–28 cm) | **Trainability** Quick to learn but can be stubborn | **Grooming** A good brushing once or twice a week | **Exercise** Plenty of play | **Likely to say** Give me a kiss! | **Unlikely to say** I'd like a nap.

Norwegian Elkhound

Late Stone Age remains suggest that this breed has been around for thousands of years. It is a strong, sturdy dog with a thick gray coat and was once used to hunt moose and bears. Its name comes from the Norwegian word *elghund*, which actually means "moose dog." The Norwegians would send these dogs to find moose. Once they did, they would bark loudly to let the hunter know they had found one. The elkhound is known for its loud and carrying bark, and its excellent tracking abilities mean it is used as a search and rescue dog.

Life expectancy 12–15 years | **Height** 19–21 in (48–53 cm) | **Trainability** Have lots of treats ready! | **Grooming** Needs weekly brushing | **Exercise** Long daily walks | **Likely to say** I found it first! | **Unlikely to say** Your wish is my command.

Swedish Vallhund

Did the Vikings take some Welsh dogs home with them when they returned to Scandinavia, or did the Vikings bring some of their dogs to Wales? This is the question, because Sweden's stocky little dog looks very much like the Welsh corgi and has the same herding instincts. Whichever way round it was, for sheer entertainment value, it's hard to beat a vallhund. These dogs were bred to work on farms in their native Sweden, and they are intelligent and quick to learn. But they have a sense of humor and will play games purely, it seems, to make you laugh.

....

Life expectancy 12–15 years | **Height** 11–14 in (28–36 cm) | **Trainability** Smart, alert, and attentive | **Grooming** Weekly brushing | **Exercise** Playful and energetic, likes to be active | **Likely to say** Watch this! | **Unlikely to say** Let's stay on the sofa all day.

Canadian Inuit Dog

Thought to be one of North America's oldest purebred indigenous dogs, the Canadian Inuit dog has been around for at least two thousand years. It was first used by the Inuit people to find seal-breathing holes in the ice, to keep polar bears at bay, to hunt, and to pull sleds across Arctic snowfields. It is said that a Canadian Inuit dog can pull twice its weight and still cover up to 70 miles (113 kilometers) per day, so you'll need a lot of stamina if this is the dog for you. It is also a pack animal, so may cause issues with other pets. Despite this, it can be charmingly playful and is very vocal—it likes to sing!

Life expectancy 10–15 years | **Height** 20–28 in (51–71 cm) | **Trainability** Quick to learn, with a great memory | **Grooming** Daily brushing | **Exercise** At least two hours a day | **Likely to say** Can we go on a long trek? | **Unlikely to say** I want to play with the cat.

Basset Hound

The instantly recognizable basset hound is a dog that seems to have been designed by several people, all with a different plan! It has short, stubby legs; a very long back (it's an ideal pet for families because everyone can pat it at once!); a sad face; and low-set, drooping ears. But despite its mournful appearance, bassets are hunters; those loose folds of skin on its face trap the scent it is sniffing out. When not following a scent, bassets love lazing about and eating. But be warned, if left alone for long, their booming howl, called a bay, will carry enough to upset the neighbors!

Life expectancy 12–13 years | **Height** Up to 15 in (Up to 38 cm) | **Trainability** Stubborn | **Grooming** Little, but wipe mouth and face | **Exercise** Prone to putting on weight, so frequent walks needed | **Likely to say** *Sniff*—he went that way! | **Unlikely to say** I don't want seconds.

Bernese Mountain Dog

Thisbreed takes its name from Bern in Switzerland, where the dog was used to herd sheep and cattle. But that wasn't all—it was pretty much an all-around farmhand! The Bernese mountain dog (also known as a Berner) was also used to pull carts carrying cheese and milk to market. A strong and striking breed, it has a black-and-tan coat with a white mark on its chest that is said to represent the Swiss flag. The Berner is an affectionate creature and always eager to please, but it doesn't like being left alone for long—and a bored Berner is likely to be a barker.

Life expectancy 7–10 years | **Height** 23–28 in (58–71 cm) | **Trainability** Easy | **Grooming** Weekly brushing | **Exercise** At least thirty minutes a day | **Likely to say** What would you like me to do next? | **Unlikely to say** No, not doing that.

Schnauzer

If you're not keen on the doggy smell (though to some it's like perfume!) the schnauzer might be a good option. When groomed and taken care of correctly, this is a breed that typically doesn't produce much of an odor. With a soft undercoat and wiry topcoat, it doesn't shed much either. With arched eyebrows and a distinct beard and mustache, the schnauzer has an aristocratic air. It comes in three sizes: miniature, standard, and giant. It is a loyal breed and has a sweet temper, but it is lively and has a booming bark—great if you're looking for a dog who can let you know of an intruder, not so great if you want to keep the neighbors happy.

....

Life expectancy 13–16 years | **Height** 12–28 in (30–71 cm) | **Trainability** Intelligent but easily bored | **Grooming** Daily brushing |
Exercise At least an hour a day—a high-energy breed | **Likely to say** WOOF! | **Unlikely to say** I can amuse myself for a while.

English Foxhound

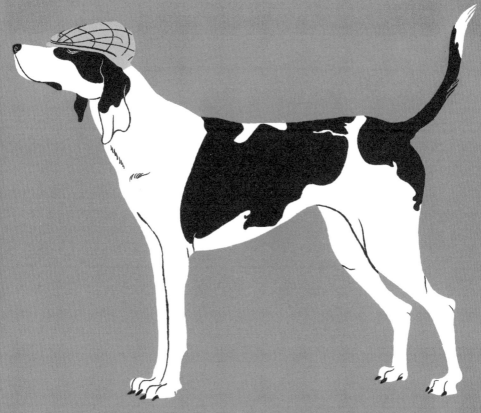

With its keen nose, bright eyes, and constantly waving stern (tail), the foxhound is a finely tuned hunting machine. It has been bred specially for these qualities for hundreds of years. The foxhound is used to working in a pack, so some do not settle very well as pets. Those that do, though, are devoted, loyal, and highly sociable. And the breed is certainly good-looking. Foxhounds are considered by many to be ideal dogs and were once described with this praise: "Next to an old Greek statue, there are few such combinations of grace and strength as a fine Foxhound."

Life expectancy 10–13 years | **Height** 24 in (61 cm) | **Trainability** Intelligent but can be stubborn | **Grooming** Weekly brushing | **Exercise** Very active | **Likely to say** I love all your friends! | **Unlikely to say** I wouldn't dream of chasing that squirrel.

Corgi

There are two types of corgis: the Cardigan and the Pembroke. Both are named for places in Wales, and the Cardigan is thought to be the elder. The name of the breed comes from the Celtic words *cor*, meaning "dwarf," and *gi*, meaning "dog." It was also known as the "yard dog" because the measurement from the tip of its nose to the end of its tail was a Welsh yard—40 inches (102 centimeters). The corgi is a tough little bundle of energy whose short legs helped it to herd cattle, which is what it was bred for. It does so less nowadays, but it likes to eat, so needs plenty of exercise.

Life expectancy Cardigan 12–15 years; Pembroke 12–13 years | **Height** Cardigan 10–13 in (25–33 cm); Pembroke 12–13 in (30–33 cm) | **Trainability** Very smart | **Grooming** Daily brushing | **Exercise** Daily walks to work off its food! | **Likely to say** Is it dinnertime yet? | **Unlikely to say** Wait for me!

Bloodhound

This sad-looking breed holds the Guinness World Record as the first animal whose "evidence" was allowed to be given in a court of law! Bloodhounds have been used to track human scent since Roman times, and their scenting ability is three hundred times better than our own. They are still used in legal cases and in search and rescue missions today, but their patience and sweet temper means they make devoted family pets, too. That's if you don't mind too much slobber! Although they're not considered particularly vocal, they do have a distinctive deep howl.

....

Life expectancy 10–12 years | **Height** 23–27 in (58–69 cm) | **Trainability** Can be stubborn | **Grooming** Weekly brushing but constant wiping! | **Exercise** Long daily runs or walks | **Likely to say** Slobber, drooool | **Unlikely to say** Should we just go around the block?

Ibizan Hound

With its elegant face and large, pricked ears, the Ibizan hound bears a strong resemblance to dogs seen on ancient Egyptian tombs, suggesting it has been around for a long time. On the Spanish islands of Ibiza and Formentera, the dogs—known as Beezers—were used to hunt rabbits and small game. It has a strong prey drive and can leap up high from a standstill, so anything on your kitchen counter is not safe. The Beezer can be a little couch potato, too. When it's not counter surfing for food or chasing small creatures, it's quite happy to curl up for a snuggle.

Life expectancy 11–14 years | Height 22–28 in (56–71 cm) | Trainability Never loses that urge to chase | Grooming Weekly brushing | Exercise A few walks a day | Likely to say Look, rabbit! | Unlikely to say I've had my dinner, I don't want anything else.

Newfoundland

Have you ever seen a dog go fishing? The Newfoundland, named for the coastal region of Canada where it came from, helped fishermen pull in their nets. Big and strong, it would also jump from boats to retrieve lost equipment and could pull heavy carts. The Newfoundland has an oily, waterproof coat and webbed feet, and today is used to rescue swimmers in distress. It was made famous in literature as Nana, the gentle and loving dog owned by the Darling family in the Peter Pan stories. The Newfie certainly lives up to its fictional counterpart as a sweet and patient pet.

Life expectancy 9–10 years | **Height** 26–29 in (66–74 cm) | **Trainability** Eager to learn | **Grooming** Brushing two or three times a week | **Exercise** Needs plenty of exercise and play | **Likely to say** What would you like me to do now? | **Unlikely to say** I don't have time for this.

Dachshund

The dachshund is everyone's favorite wiener dog. Its name means "badger dog" in German, as it was once used to hunt badgers as well as rabbits and even wild boar. The journalist H.L. Mencken once described the breed as "half a dog high and a dog and a half long," which, when you see a doxie, looks about right! As they were bred to go down into burrows, their barrel-like chest contains large lungs to help them breathe underground. They have a loud bark for a little dog, so be warned! Despite their hunting past, the doxie—in both miniature and standard sizes—makes a lively pet.

Life expectancy 12–16 years | **Height** 5–9 in (13–23 cm) | **Trainability** Quite stubborn | **Grooming** Occasional brushing but clean ears often | **Exercise** Walks and play needed | **Likely to say** What are you doing and can I help? | **Unlikely to say** No way I'm going down there!

Puli

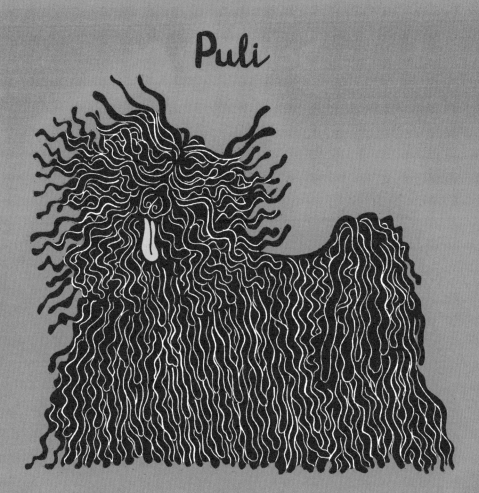

The puli is famous for its extraordinary coat. Its hair forms long twisted cords as it grows, keeping the puli warm and protecting its skin. In its native Hungary, the puli was a herding dog, and under all that hair is a swift and nimble animal. Its coat comes in a variety of colors, including black—the color preferred by Hungarian shepherds, who could easily detect the dog among the sheep! As a pet it is loving and playful, but has never forgotten its herding roots and remains protective.

Life expectancy 10–15 years | **Height** 16–17 in (41–43 cm) | **Trainability** Clever, but easily distracted | **Grooming** Specialist needed to help to keep the cords in order | **Exercise** Needs lots | **Likely to say** I'm bored. | **Unlikely to say** Can someone brush my hair?

Schipperke

This breed's nickname is LBD—little black devil! Its actual name means "little skipper" because this dog was used as a watchdog on barges that traveled the canals across Belgium. It still thinks it's a watchdog today and will bark at strangers, so some people might be less than enchanted. But the schipperke is bright and mischievous and has a sense of humor; its foxy face and big smile may just win you over. This intelligent breed has also been used as a service dog, in search and rescue missions, and for sniffing out drugs and explosives. It can be aloof with strangers but is devoted to its family.

Life expectancy 12–16 years | Height 10–13 in (25–33 cm) | Trainability Clever but has its own ideas | Grooming Weekly brushing | Exercise Needs up to an hour a day | Likely to say Aye, aye, cap'n. | Unlikely to say Come on in!

Dalmatian

Instantly recognizable with its black spots, and made famous by the movie *101 Dalmatians*, this breed was known as the "spotted coach dog." Something of a status symbol, the Dalmatian would trot alongside coaches to protect them from highwaymen by day, acting as watchdogs at rest stops by night. It would also run ahead of fire engines, clearing their path to the inferno. In the United States, fire stations traditionally had a "fire dog" as a mascot and many still do today. The Dalmatian has an endearing nature and thinks everyone is its friend, but it can be too lively for some.

....

Life expectancy 11–13 years | **Height** 19–24 in (48–61 cm) | **Trainability** Eager to please | **Grooming** Sheds a lot so plenty of brushing | **Exercise** More than two hours a day | **Likely to say** Let's go out! Let's go to the park! | **Unlikely to say** I'm going to take a nap.

Lagotto Romagnolo

Although its name means "curly-coated duck retriever from Romango," this Italian water dog no longer retrieves ducks since the marshes of its homeland were drained at the beginning of the twentieth century. It is now the only dog that is bred to hunt truffles—its keen nose sniffing out delicacies while its thick, curly fur keeps it warm. But there is much more to the Lagotto—that curly coat makes it an ideal pet for those who suffer with allergies, and it is affectionate, loyal, and eager to please. Just remember that it likes to dig!

Life expectancy 15–17 years | **Height** 16–19 in (41–48 cm) | **Trainability** Quick learner | **Grooming** A few times a week | **Exercise** More than two hours a day | **Likely to say** This smells like a good spot. | **Unlikely to say** I will never dig up your flower beds.

Great Dane

It's hardly surprising that this noble giant is known as the "Apollo of dogs." Apollo is the Greek god of the sun, and few breeds shine brighter. Despite its name, the Great Dane has closer links with Germany than Denmark, where it was used to hunt wild boar. Unsurprisingly, this huge dog doesn't lack courage, and its sheer good looks meant nobility chose this breed as their companion dogs. Despite its size, the Great Dane is gentle and kind, excellent with children, but a serious deterrent for any burglar. Well, would you be brave enough to try and get past one?

Life expectancy 7–10 years | **Height** 28–32 in (71–81 cm) | **Trainability** Likes to please but needs patience | **Grooming** Once a week | **Exercise** An hour a day but lots of space to roam | **Likely to say** What shall we do next? | **Unlikely to say** I don't want to play with you.

Beagle

This scent hound has been described as a "nose with legs." Incredibly, the beagle's nose holds around 220 million scent receptors compared with our paltry 5 million or so. It is the smallest of Great Britain's scent hounds and has been used on hunting expeditions since the fourteenth century. Although similar in appearance to the foxhound, they may make better pets. It's a pack animal and sticks to its owner like glue. The most famous beagle is Snoopy, who has a fixation with his food bowl. This is art imitating life—beagles love their grub and will eat everything!

....

Life expectancy 10–15 years | **Height** 13–15 in (33–38 cm) | **Trainability** Can be stubborn but will do anything for food | **Grooming** Weekly brushing and keep ears clean | **Exercise** At least one hour a day | **Likely to say** *Sniff, sniff, sniff* . . . | **Unlikely to say** Can't smell a thing.

Maremmano-Abruzzese Sheepdog

Like most sheepdogs, this Italian version is very good at its job and is happiest doing it. The ancestors to this mixed breed are known to go back to Roman times—if not even further. It is an independent thinker and tends to bond with the flock it's protecting—a job it takes very seriously. That tendency to guard has even saved penguins! Maremmano-Abruzzeses were used to guard a population of little penguins on a tiny Australian island near the coastal town of Warrnambool. Where other animals had failed, this dog succeeded in keeping red foxes at bay, and the penguin colony thrived.

Life expectancy 11–13 years | **Height** 23–29 in (59–73 cm) | **Trainability** A little too independent | **Grooming** Lots of brushing | **Exercise** Needs long and interesting walks | **Likely to say** Who are you and what do you want? | **Unlikely to say** Come on in!

Bichon Frisé

If you want a happy little dog that will adore you, go for the bichon frisé! *Bichon* means "lapdog" and *frisé* refers to the corkscrew curls of its soft, fluffy coat. Add black eyes, a button nose, and an air of mischief to sum up this delightful breed. The bichon frisé is thought to have come from Tenerife in the Canary Islands, perhaps as long ago as the fourteenth century, but it was developed into the modern dog in France, where it was popular with nobility. Despite its size, the bichon is quite hardy and is always cheerful—the perfect companion.

....

Life expectancy 14–15 years | **Height** 9–12 in (23–30 cm) | **Trainability** Loves to learn | **Grooming** At least twice-weekly combing | **Exercise** Walks and plenty of play | **Likely to say** Check out my curls! | **Unlikely to say** I don't want to play.

Vizsla

There is something aristocratic about this handsome breed. The vizsla was developed in Hungary as a pointing and retrieving dog, and was both hardworking and good at its job. But today it is also known as the Velcro dog because it sticks to its human owner! Its favorite place to be is fastened to your side, leaning against you or lying on your feet. The vizsla is very vocal too—not a good trait if you want to get along with your neighbors. You must make sure your dog has plenty to occupy its keen and inquiring mind.

....

Life expectancy 12–14 years | **Height** 21–24 in (53–61 cm) | **Trainability** Intelligent and eager to please | **Grooming** An occasional brush or wipe with a damp cloth | **Exercise** At least an hour a day | **Likely to say** Everything, and loudly! | **Unlikely to say** Off you go, then.

Poodle

The traditional poodle cut—pom-pom tail and ankles, fluffy chest, and curly topknot—may look cute, but it once served a real purpose. The poodle was originally a water dog, or *pudelhund*, and the cut enabled it to move easily through water without getting snagged while protecting it from the cold. Although its name is German, the poodle was developed in France, where its elegance and quiet dignity made it much in demand. There are three sizes—toy, miniature, and standard—and all are highly intelligent and equally beautiful.

Life expectancy 10–18 years | **Height** Under 10 to more than 15 in (25–38 cm) | **Trainability** Easy due to high intelligence | **Grooming** High maintenance | **Exercise** Walks and plenty of play | **Likely to say** I bet I know what you're thinking. | **Unlikely to say** I need a perm.

Saint Bernard

In the tenth century, a monk founded a monastery in the Swiss Alps to care for travelers who struggled on its treacherous routes. The monastery used dogs, Alpine mastiffs, to seek fallen pilgrims in the cold and snow and lead them back to safety. Descendants of those dogs—which were bred to be bigger and stronger, perhaps with Newfoundland and bloodhound lines—are still used as search and rescue dogs today. The monastery was called Saint Bernard's, and its heroic dogs took the name. The modern Saint is gentle, quiet, and calm and, if you don't mind a bit of drool, makes a lovely pet.

Life expectancy 8–10 years | **Height** 26–30 in (66–76 cm) | **Trainability** Can be stubborn | **Grooming** Brushing three times a week | **Exercise** Surprisingly little for their size | **Likely to say** Follow me! | **Unlikely to say** I have no idea where I am.

Bedlington Terrier

At first glance, this breed looks more like a lamb than a dog! Like many terriers, the Bedlington was bred to hunt rats, and even foxes. Originally bred in the English mining town of Bedlington, this dog makes an entertaining family pet because it just loves to be the center of attention and is always happy to play the clown. The downside to this is that it prefers to be an "only dog"—it doesn't like competing with other pets. The Bedlington can be quite aggressive to strangers and will let you know if it dislikes anyone. It's said to be a great judge of character.

Life expectancy 11–16 years | **Height** 15–18 in (38–46 cm) | **Trainability** Easy to train, if it wants! | **Grooming** Weekly combing | **Exercise** Will happily match its needs to yours | **Likely to say** Look at me! | **Unlikely to say** I absolutely love your new friend.

Briard

Most dog breeds are loving, but the affectionate briard is sometimes called a "heart wrapped in fur." It's a herding breed from France, thought to date back to the eighth century, and its name is a shorter form of Chien Berger de Brie, after the region of its home country. While it's a very loving pet, the briard can be wary of strangers, which makes it an excellent guard dog as it will bark loudly—the briard likes the sound of its own voice!

Life expectancy 12 years | **Height** 22–27 in (56–69 cm) | **Trainability** A quick study but can be stubborn | **Grooming** Daily brushing | **Exercise** A long walk or run every day | **Likely to say** Let's hang out. | **Unlikely to say** Don't care who you are, come on in!

Bracco Italiano

There is a touch of bloodhound in this Italian breed, though it's used as an HPR (hunt, point, retrieve) dog rather than a scent hound. The bracco Italiano is considered to be Europe's oldest pointer; similar dogs are depicted in paintings dating back to the fourth and fifth centuries! Those long ears, endearing eyes, and noble expression make it appealing. And despite the fact that it's a working breed, the bracco makes an excellent pet. It has endless patience and a sweet temper. It rarely barks, however, so doesn't make the best guard dog.

Life expectancy 10–14 years | Height 21–27 in (53–69 cm) | Trainability Easy, but be gentle | Grooming Once a week | Exercise At least half an hour a day | Likely to say Ciao! | Unlikely to say Look! There's someone coming.

Irish Wolfhound

This giant breed can move surprisingly fast. The Irish wolfhound was used in wars to pull men off horses or chariots. In 391 CE, seven of these majestic creatures were gifted to Roman statesman Quintus Aurelius Symmachus, who wrote that: "all Rome viewed them with wonder." The wolfhound makes a great family dog because it's so gentle. But be warned: it is known to be "gentle when stroked, fierce when provoked." It's too serene to be much good as a guard dog, but its size would frighten off even the toughest burglar.

Life expectancy 6–8 years | **Height** At least 32–35 in (81–89 cm) | **Trainability** Easy but needs consistency | **Grooming** Weekly brushing | **Exercise** At least forty minutes a day | **Likely to say** I can see everything from up here! | **Unlikely to say** Come any closer and I'll bite.

German Pinscher

The German pinscher is undoubtedly the ancestor of the handsome Doberman as they share the same sleekly muscular body, pricked ears, and wedge-shaped muzzle. Intelligent, the pinscher knows when it has done something naughty, such as chewing something it shouldn't have, and will stretch its lips over its teeth in a "smile" to get back on your good side. It will take over your heart and your home in a moment.

Life expectancy 12–14 years | **Height** 17–20 in (43–51 cm) | **Trainability** Very smart | **Grooming** Weekly brushing | **Exercise** Energetic, so needs plenty of exercise | **Likely to say** Oops, sorry. | **Unlikely to say** Of *course* I won't chew your favorite shoes.

Old English Sheepdog

If you've heard something called a "shaggy-dog story," this is probably the breed to which it referred—dogs don't come much shaggier! The Old English Sheepdog's fluffy blue-and-white coat protected it from the elements. As a pet, the Old English Sheepdog is playful and comical. The American Kennel Club describes this breed as having "a distinctive bear-like gait and a mellow, agreeable nature."

....

Life expectancy 10–12 years | **Height** At least 21–22 in (53–56 cm) | **Trainability** Quick learner | **Grooming** Often, plus professional grooming | **Exercise** Lots, mental and physical | **Likely to say** Does anyone have hairspray? | **Unlikely to say** Does anyone else feel chilly?

Havanese

If this little bundle of fluff looks familiar, it's because it's thought to be related to the bichon frisé. The Havanese is the national dog of Cuba, taken there by the Spanish. That gorgeous coat looks too hot for such a climate but it is actually a bit like raw silk—fine and cool. Havanese become devoted to their owners and suffer separation anxiety, but that's a small price to pay for so much love. A warning, however: keep an eye on the toilet paper! Your Havanese thinks paper is the best toy in the world, and your house will be festooned with it, like at Halloween.

Life expectancy 14–16 years | **Height** 8–12 in (20–30 cm) | **Trainability** Very smart | **Grooming** Daily brushing and occasional baths | **Exercise** More than you'd think for such a small dog | **Likely to say** More attention, please. | **Unlikely to say** Of course I won't touch the toilet paper.

Komondor

This dog is a commanding animal in all sorts of ways. The biggest of the Hungarian herding breeds, a solid and powerful dog stands under that impressive coat. Add in a dash of courage and a lot of attitude and you have something that few people would choose to argue with. And despite its size, the kom (as it is commonly known) is surprisingly fast. It makes an exceptional guard dog and is naturally very protective. More than anything else, it's happy watching over you and your every move . . . which can be pretty unnerving! If you don't mind its constant gaze, this is the dog for you.

Life expectancy 10–12 years | **Height** At least 25–28 in (64–71 cm) | **Trainability** Intelligent but has a stubborn streak | **Grooming** Complicated! | **Exercise** Two or three walks a day | **Likely to say** Carry on, I'm just watching. | **Unlikely to say** Whatever, I'm not watching.

Collie

Thanks to the beloved 1943 film *Lassie Come Home*, the collie is one of the most recognizable dog breeds. And Lassie herself (played by a male dog, but who cares?) had all the qualities we look for in a pet. She was brave, loyal, devoted, and extremely beautiful. The breed comes from Scotland, where it was used as a herder. It guarded black-faced sheep called colleys, which is perhaps where its name comes from. Intelligent and sensitive, the collie is playful and gentle, especially with children, but can be very protective of its human "herd."

Life expectancy 12–14 years | **Height** 22–26 in (56–66 cm) | **Trainability** Learns easily | **Grooming** Thorough brushing | **Exercise** A brisk daily walk and lots of play | **Likely to say** Everyone in the kitchen, now! | **Unlikely to say** Go out and leave me, I'll be fine.

Boxer

A great, joyful, boisterous bundle of energy, the boxer was originally a guard dog, but is now more popular as a pet. It is high-energy and wants to be involved in everything you do, but retains a lovable puppyish charm well into adulthood. The boxer is not considered mature until it is three years old. A happy boxer—and they are nearly always happy—twists its body in a dance known as the kidney bean, named for the semi-circular shape it makes. It also makes a delightful *woo-woo* sound—you will always know when your boxer is excited.

Life expectancy 10–12 years | Height 21–25 in (53–64 cm) | Trainability Eager to please—but don't let it get away with anything! | Grooming Weekly brushing | Exercise Lots, both physical and mental | Likely to say I love everything! | Unlikely to say I'm unhappy.

West Highland White Terrier

Also known as the Westie, this little dog has a large dollop of self-esteem. It has all the terrier traits—sturdy, tough, brave, assertive—but is very much its own "person." The Westie also has the terrier tenacity—once onto something, such as a rabbit or a squirrel, it will pursue it with single-minded determination. Apart from a tendency to be bossy with other pets, the Westie is a cheerful and devoted companion, though it likes to be included in everything and is something of a busybody. It likes everybody and welcomes all with a waving tail.

Life expectancy 13–15 years | Height 10–11 in (25–28 cm) | Trainability Quick to learn | Grooming The occasional wipe-down and the odd bath | Exercise Daily runs and lots of play | Likely to say What's in it for me? | Unlikely to say You can't come in.

Irish Setter

With a coat that glows golden-red in the sunlight, the Irish setter is one of the most glamorous breeds. It was bred to work as a bird dog (a gun-dog trained to retrieve birds) and was a determined and driven hunter. It was also known as the red setter, to separate it from the Irish red-and-white setter, but it differs in other ways too; it is finer boned, with a more chiseled head. As a pet, it is full of energy and always up for a game, but that ecstatic bounce can be a little overwhelming for some. Be prepared for a lot of fun!

....

Life expectancy 12–15 years | **Height** 25–27 in (63–68 cm) | **Trainability** Quick to learn—if not distracted! | **Grooming** Daily brushing | **Exercise** At least an hour a day | **Likely to say** Be sure to get my best side. | **Unlikely to say** I'm not in the mood to have fun.

Bull Terrier

The bull terrier is handsome in its own way, with a noble profile and charming smile. It was bred as a fighting dog, probably through a cross between a bulldog and the now extinct English white terrier. It was then known as a bull-and-terrier. But the modern version is a lover, not a fighter. It is affectionate and friendly, loves its family, and is always delighted to play the class clown to make you laugh. It has been referred to as the "kid in a dog suit" for its playful and happy personality.

....

Life expectancy 12–13 years | Height 21–22 in (53–56 cm) | Trainability Can be a challenge | Grooming Weekly brushing | Exercise Between thirty to sixty minutes a day due to terrier energy | Likely to say Let's play! | Unlikely to say I'm too tired.

American Cocker Spaniel

Given this little dog's beauty, it's hardly surprising that it was the most popular breed of pet in the United States for more than a decade. While some consider the English version to be the same as the US one, the American Kennel Club recognized them as two separate breeds in 1946. They certainly share the same melting brown eyes, soft ears, and silky coat. But while the English cocker is still very much a working dog, the American cocker is far more likely to be found on the show bench, or simply enjoying life as a family pet, receiving all the love and attention it deserves.

Life expectancy 10–14 years | **Height** 13–16 in (33–41 cm) | **Trainability** A people pleaser! | **Grooming** Regular brushing | **Exercise** Lots of walks and playtime | **Likely to say** What would you like me to do? | **Unlikely to say** I'm not doing that.

Boston Terrier

This delightful little dog looks like it's dressed in a tux ready for a night on the town! That smart tuxedo-like marking earned the breed the nickname the "American gentleman." It was also previously known as a bull terrier and roundhead. The Boston terrier is bustling, busy, bossy, and inquisitive (all the terrier characteristics in one) and, with its erect ears and large eyes, can charm just about anyone. Though small, it is sturdy and enjoys a bit of rough play, so it makes a great pet for children. Like many terriers, it can have a stubborn streak, but food can be a great motivator!

....

Life expectancy 11–13 years | **Height** 10–12 in (25–30 cm) | **Trainability** Smart but stubborn | **Grooming** Very little | **Exercise** | Daily walks | **Likely to say** Watch me! | **Unlikely to say** I don't feel like playing with you.

English Cocker Spaniel

The English cocker is different from the American version, largely because it is still a working breed. A member of the land spaniel subgroup, this dog was originally used to hunt birds like woodcock, hence the name. The land spaniel grouping was decided by size and weight, and the cocker was any spaniel that weighed less than 24 pounds (11 kilograms). Recorded as a separate breed since 1893, it is still in demand in the shooting field, but has long been popular as a family pet for its loving nature and merry demeanor. The happily waving tail of a cocker will always make you smile.

Life expectancy 12–14 years | **Height** 15–17 in (38–43 cm) | **Trainability** Eager to please but needs gentle handling | **Grooming** Daily, or book a groomer! | **Exercise** Needs an hour a day | **Likely to say** Look, pheasant! | **Unlikely to say** I'm sad.

Affenpinscher

Less a dog, more a cartoon Tasmanian devil! This extraordinary breed gets its name from the German word *Affen* (monkey). The French call it the *diablotin moustachu*, or "mustached little devil." But those who know the breed all agree on one point—the affenpinscher is a cheeky, adorable, entertaining clown, and those who have one say they love their little monkey. As with many breeds, it's hard to know who owns whom!

Life expectancy 12–15 years | **Height** 9–12 in (23–30 cm) | **Trainability** Smart, but can be willful | **Grooming** Occasional brushing | **Exercise** Best suited for short, brisk walks | **Likely to say** It wasn't me. | **Unlikely to say** Stop! Who are you?

Spinone Italiano

One of the oldest hunting breeds in the world, the modern spinone's calm and sweet nature means it makes the perfect pet for a family. It adores children and likes to be involved in all play or other activities. But it doesn't do to forget its hunting past; the spinone may find passing cats and other small animals extremely interesting. The name *spinone* comes from the Italian word for "prickly," perhaps in reference to its wiry coat, which protects it when it's hunting in dense thorny bushes. But if you choose a spinone Italiano, it will never be a thorn in your side.

. . . .

Life expectancy 10–12 years | **Height** 22–27 in (56–69 cm) | **Trainability** Easy, unless it sees a cat! | **Grooming** Brushing a few times a week | **Exercise** At least an hour a day | **Likely to say** Let's play! | **Unlikely to say** I haven't noticed that cat.

Hamiltonstövare

Thought to be the result of crossing an English foxhound with German hounds, this hunting dog was developed in Sweden by Count Adolf Hamilton, hence the name. But unlike foxhounds, the Hamiltonstövare was bred to hunt singly, rather than in packs, and was used to pursue fox, deer, and wild boar. It's a handsome breed, with a tricolor coat of black, tan, and white. Though the Hamiltonstövare can be kept as a pet, it tends to be boisterous, so it's not ideal around children. And it retains its prey drive, so must be well trained or it will take off in pursuit of any small animal.

Life expectancy 14–17 years | **Height** 19–24 in (48–61 cm) | **Trainability** Intelligent but can be stubborn | **Grooming** Weekly brushing | **Exercise** Lots of walks and playtime | **Likely to say** RABBIT! | **Unlikely to say** I just want to lie on the sofa and snooze.

Leonberger

Looking at this giant breed, it's no surprise that the Leonberger was developed using Newfoundland, Saint Bernard, and Great Pyrenees bloodlines. Its fierce appearance is misleading, though, because it is gentle, loving, and sensitive. The breed was created by Heinrich Essig, mayor of the town of Leonberg in southern Germany, because he wanted a lionlike dog to match the lions on the town's heraldic crest. Leonbergers were used as guard dogs—their size and deep bark would make a potential burglar think twice—but their sweet natures mean they make lovely family pets.

....

Life expectancy 7 years | **Height** 25–32 in (64–81 cm) | **Trainability** Intelligent and eager to please | **Grooming** Brushing at least once a week | **Exercise** Lots | **Likely to say** Please don't fight, love me instead. | **Unlikely to say** I don't like you.

Pumi

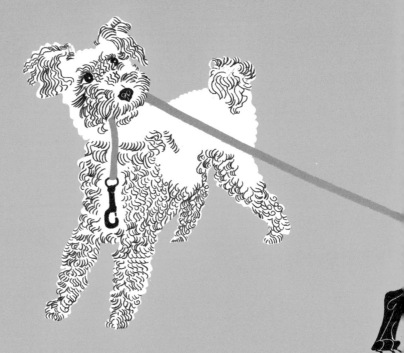

This delightful character was developed using its Hungarian cousin, the puli. The pumi is a herding dog and is extremely tough and hardy as well as swift. It was used to move semi-wild flocks along the narrow trails between the pastures of western Hungary, but its undeniable charm did not go unnoticed. The pumi's corkscrew curls and sweet expression don't mislead; it has a cheerful nature and an appealing desire to please. But pumik (the plural of pumi) are not for everyone: they need lots of exercise and attention, and preferably a task to do around the house, as they are easily bored.

....

Life expectancy 12–13 years | **Height** 15–19 in (38–48 cm) | **Trainability** Intelligent, but has its own mind | **Grooming** Occasional brushing | **Exercise** Lots, and ideally outdoors | **Likely to say** Can I help you with that? | **Unlikely to say** No, I don't want to go outside.

German Shepherd

It was during World War I that the handsome German shepherd really gained recognition for its courage and calm temperament. Since then it has had many jobs, being used by both the police and armed forces, as a guide dog, and as a therapy dog. Known as the GSD for short, it is also sometimes called the Alsatian (it comes from Alsace-Lorraine, along the border of Germany and France). There are two varieties, shorthaired and longhaired. If you fall in love with the longhaired GSD, beware: it leaves hair everywhere. It is sometimes known as the "German shedder."

Life expectancy 7–10 years | Height 22–26 in (56–66 cm) | Trainability Intelligent and eager to learn | Grooming Frequent brushing | Exercise Needs lots of walks and runs | Likely to say Halt! Who goes there? | Unlikely to say Please brush me.

Jack Russell Terrier

Historically, the British clergy were fond of hunting, and this breed was developed by Parson John "Jack" Russell, largely to go down holes and flush out quarry (rats, rabbits, or even foxes). Russell shaped a terrier that was brave, intelligent, athletic, fast, and determined and that possessed a great hunting drive. That's not to say the Jack Russell doesn't make a good family pet; they are affectionate and loyal. But their potential for mischief is massive. They love to chew anything, from phones to passports, and have been known to scarf down whatever they can get their paws on.

....

Life expectancy 12–14 years | **Height** 10–12 in (25–31 cm) | **Trainability** Smart but can be stubborn | **Grooming** Weekly brushing | **Exercise** Up to forty-five minutes a day | **Likely to say** That looks tasty. | **Unlikely to say** I promise I won't chew it.

Border Collie

Named for the borders between England, Scotland, and Wales, this herding dog is renowned for its sharp brain and sleek speed. It is also known for its "eye"—an intense stare that allows it to note even the slightest change in its flock. Though the border collie is still in demand as a superb sheepdog all over the world, it is a popular pet, too. But if you want a cuddly couch potato, this is not the breed for you. The border collie needs plenty of exercise and its brain must be stimulated or it will become bored, unhappy, and destructive. This dog needs a job to do!

Life expectancy 12–15 years | **Height** 18–22 in (46–56 cm) | **Trainability** Easy, it loves to learn | **Grooming** Weekly brushing | **Exercise** Plenty, it needs something to think about | **Likely to say** Be right back! | **Unlikely to say** I don't feel like it today.

Doberman Pinscher

With its erect ears, long muzzle, and muscular build, the Doberman is an aristocratic breed. But its original purpose was pretty humble; it was developed by a tax collector named Karl Friedrich Louis Dobermann around 1890 in Germany as a guard dog. Since then, it has been used by the police and armed forces, as a tracking dog, and still as a guard dog. Because the Doberman is intelligent and trainable, it can fulfill a variety of roles, including that of a family pet. They can be gentle and affectionate, but you must make sure they know you are the leader of the "pack" or they will take over!

Life expectancy 10–12 years | **Height** 24–28 in (61–71 cm) | **Trainability** Smart and eager to learn | **Grooming** Weekly brushing | **Exercise** Energetic, so lots! | **Likely to say** Come with me! | **Unlikely to say** Do come in.

Black Russian Terrier

The word *terrier* is misleading; this breed—also known as Russia's "black pearl"—is a large dog. It was developed by the Russian army after World War II as a guard dog, and one of its duties was to round up fugitives. After two wars, there were few dogs left in Russia, so the new breed was created using the giant schnauzer, Airedale terrier, and Rottweiler, with a dash of something known as the Moscow terrier. The modern breed is attractive and devoted to its owner, and retains its protective instincts. You'll always feel safe with your "black pearl."

....

Life expectancy 10–12 years | **Height** 26–30 in (66–76 cm) | **Trainability** Smart but bossy | **Grooming** Lots—you'll need a brush and a comb | **Exercise** Lots of runs and games | **Likely to say** Who goes there? | **Unlikely to say** Don't worry, I won't chase you.

Sealyham Terrier

Captain John Tucker-Edwardes of Pembrokeshire, Wales, initially developed this cheerful terrier to hunt alongside his otterhounds. Edwardes wanted a compact, short-legged dog that would be small enough to go to ground after otter, badger, fox, or polecat—and brave enough to want to! When he had the type of dog he wanted, Edwardes named it after his home, Sealyham Manor. The modern Sealyham is the clown of the terrier world; it has a great sense of humor and is always up for a game. But beware—fans of the Sealy say they are a little like chips . . . one is never enough.

Life expectancy 12–14 years | Height 11 in (28 cm) | Trainability Can be stubborn | Grooming Brushing three times a week | Exercise An hour a day | Likely to say Watch me do this! | Unlikely to say I don't like being laughed at.

Labrador Retriever

It is hardly surprising that the Labrador retriever has been on the favorite dog breed lists for decades. Usually referred to as a Labrador or, more affectionately, a Lab, this handsome and clever dog comes from Canada, where it was a fishermen's helper, hauling in nets and lines and even retrieving fish. It was originally known as the St. John's dog, after the capital city of Newfoundland. Brought to England around 1800, it became the go-to gundog for retrieving shot birds. But its gentle and loving nature makes it a perfect family pet. Its only downfall is greed; the Lab loves to eat!

Life expectancy 11–13 years | **Height** 21–25 in (53–64 cm) | **Trainability** Always eager to learn | **Grooming** Daily brushing—Labs shed! | **Exercise** Daily walks of at least thirty minutes | **Likely to say** Can I eat that? | **Unlikely to say** I'm not hungry, thanks.

Nederlandse Kooikerhondje

The Nederlandse kooikerhondje (*koi-ker-hond-yuh*) is known as the little white-and-orange dog with a big heart. Called the kooiker, this attractive breed comes from the Netherlands, where it has been used since the sixteenth century as a hunting dog. Its gaily waving tail would lure ducks into the hunters' nets. It has a place in history, as it was a kooiker who alerted Britain's William of Orange to intruders by barking loudly, saving his life. An attractive dog, the kooiker can make a devoted pet, but it is a little bundle of energy and needs to be mentally stimulated.

Life expectancy 12–15 years | **Height** 15–16 in (38–41 cm) | **Trainability** Smart and eager to learn | **Grooming** Weekly brushing | **Exercise** Lots—it's no couch potato | **Likely to say** Let's go! | **Unlikely to say** I'd like to take a nap.

Weimaraner

Also known as the "silver ghost" for its beautiful gray coat and pale eyes, the Weimaraner was created at the German Court of Weimar for the nobility and used to hunt. It was so highly prized that German aristocracy formed an owners' club, and if a Weimaraner was sold to a non-member, it was secretly sterilized in order to keep the breed elite. It was only after World War II that Weimaraners became known to the wider world, and they were, for a period, the most expensive dog in the world. It is demanding but is utterly devoted—as well as "silver ghost," it is often nicknamed "shadow."

Life expectancy 10–13 years | **Height** 23–27 in (58–68 cm) | **Trainability** Can be challenging and needs patience | **Grooming** Weekly brushing | **Exercise** Two hours a day | **Likely to say** Aren't I beautiful? | **Unlikely to say** No, I don't want to come with you.

Dandie Dinmont Terrier

A character in a novel by Sir Walter Scott gave this charming terrier its equally charming name. It's fitting that this is the only breed with permission to wear an official Scottish clan tartan. Alert and friendly, this devoted canine is calmer than most terriers, and it is often styled with a distinctive topknot of silky hair on its head. Today, the Dandie is becoming rare, with less than a hundred registered in 2018, but it has a devoted fan base who value its quiet dignity and intelligence.

Life expectancy 12–15 years | Height 8–11 in (20–28 cm) | Trainability Clever but gets bored easily | Grooming Brushing two or three times a week | Exercise Daily walks and play | Likely to say I'm bored. | Unlikely to say I'll do whatever you'd like me to!

English Setter

Setters get their name from their habit of crouching low—or "setting"—when they find prey such as birds, so hunters can throw nets over whatever they find. Beautiful and graceful creatures, they are still used as gundogs and prized for their work ethic, but they also make great pets. The English setter is affectionate and gentle, and it is utterly devoted to its family. It makes an excellent guard dog, too, but once introduced will accept any guest calmly and happily. It is a great breed for the first-time dog owner.

....

Life expectancy 12 years | **Height** 23–27 in (58–68 cm) | **Trainability** Needs firm kindness | **Grooming** Daily brushing advised | **Exercise** Lots of room to run around | **Likely to say** Welcome! | **Unlikely to say** No, you can't come in.

English Springer Spaniel

At one point, springer and cocker spaniels were considered the same breed. While the cocker was used to hunt wading birds such as woodcock, the springer would spring into the air to flush out game birds, which would then be captured by a hunter's hawk or, before guns were invented, caught under a tossed net. But spaniels have been around for a long time, and dogs looking very much like the English springer can be seen in sixteenth- and seventeenth-century artwork. The springer is still used as a gundog today, but it also makes a wonderful family pet because it has a sweet nature and is gentle and affectionate.

Life expectancy 12–14 years | **Height** 9–22 in (48–56 cm) | **Trainability** Intelligent but willful | **Grooming** Brushing three times a week | **Exercise** Daily walks but on the leash | **Likely to say** Bird! | **Unlikely to say** I won't chase that pigeon, I promise.

Staffordshire Bull Terrier

The Staffordshire bull terrier gets its name because of its origins in Staffordshire, England. There are several dog breeds that have had bad press, and the sweet Staffy is one of them. It shares some common heritage with the English bulldog and it too was developed as a fighting dog. This can be seen in its broad face, muscular body, and powerful stance. Thankfully its fighting days are long over, and the Staffy is now in demand as a pet because it is brave, intelligent, and affectionate. A happy dog, it remains delightfully playful well into adulthood.

Life expectancy 12–14 years | **Height** 14–16 in (35–41 cm) | **Trainability** Intelligent but you must be firm and consistent | **Grooming** Weekly brushing | **Exercise** Lots of walks and runs | **Likely to say** What shall we play now? | **Unlikely to say** Wanna fight?

Kerry Blue Terrier

This is the everyman terrier. Bred in County Kerry in Ireland, the Kerry blue was used to hunt small mammals and birds, rats, and otters, as well as herd sheep and cattle. Its gorgeous silky coat gives the breed its name, though puppies are born black and turn "blue" at around eighteen months old. It has all the feisty spirit you'd expect from a terrier. Although it can be strong-willed, its friendly nature and intelligence means it makes a great family dog, though it doesn't always get along with other pets. The blue is also an excellent guard dog—its bark is impressive!

....

Life expectancy 12–15 years | Height 17–20 in (43–51 cm) | Trainability Intelligent but strong-willed | Grooming Daily brushing |
Exercise Lots—an active dog | Likely to say Can we get rid of the cat? | Unlikely to say Oh lovely, we're getting another puppy.

Rottweiler

Rotties—as they are known—are the multitaskers of the dog world. A German breed, the Rottweiler was used to drive cattle to market, as well as to pull carts of meat for butchers. There was a thriving livestock market in the southwestern German city of Rottweil, which gave the breed its name. The farmers and butchers would use their powerful dogs to guard their herd or their goods, as well as carry money bags around their neck. Later, Rottweilers were among the earliest police dogs. Brave and reliable, strong and enduring, the Rottweiler is still held in high regard.

Life expectancy 9–10 years | **Height** 22–27 in (56–69 cm) | **Trainability** Needs to know who's boss | **Grooming** Weekly brushing | **Exercise** A few twenty-minute walks a day | **Likely to say** I will protect you. | **Unlikely to say** You're on your own, I'm scared.

Border Terrier

Hardworking and keen, this bright-eyed little dog ran alongside foxhounds to flush out foxes on the borders of England and Scotland, hence the name. It was also known as the Reedwater terrier and the Coquetdale terrier. While still very much a working breed, the border's lively spirit and terrier charm means it is as much in demand as a companion. But those terrier traits means it can be challenging—it's an escape artist and has never lost its strong prey drive. The border terrier is a whirlwind of destructive energy if bored.

Life expectancy 12–15 years | **Height** 12–15 in (30–38 cm) | **Trainability** Independent but eager to please | **Grooming** Weekly brushing | **Exercise** At least half an hour a day, and plenty of play | **Likely to say** I'm bored. | **Unlikely to say** Nope, I don't want to play.

Large Münsterländer

Smart in its distinctive black and white, the Münsterländer is a large, versatile gundog from Germany. It is thought to have its ancestry in longhaired retrieving and pointing dogs found across Europe. Art from the sixteenth and seventeenth centuries depicts animals very similar to the modern breed. As with many of the gundog breeds, the Münsterländer is as good a companion as it is a worker since it is cheerful, courageous, obedient, and loyal. But it's a dog that loves to be outside, so is not ideal for apartment or city living.

....

Life expectancy 12–14 years | **Height** 20–27 in (51–69 cm) | **Trainability** Intelligent, but easily bored | **Grooming** Frequent brushing | **Exercise** A brisk daily walk and playtime | **Likely to say** Let's go outside! | **Unlikely to say** I don't feel like going out today.

Fox Terrier

Loving and playful, this tough little dog can make a loyal and devoted companion. But never forget it is a terrier first and foremost, so mischief is its middle name. The fox terrier was originally used to bolt foxes from their dens and drive them toward the huntsman. There were two varieties, smooth-haired and wire-haired; the smooth was prized because it was less likely to be mistaken for a fox, but the wire-haired dogs could push through thick vegetation. While they are popular and charming pets, their prey drive and love for digging can make them challenging.

....

Life expectancy 12–15 years | **Height** 16 in (41 cm) | **Trainability** Intelligent but strong-willed | **Grooming** Regular brushing | **Exercise** Plenty of stimulation | **Likely to say** That looks a like a good spot for digging. | **Unlikely to say** I don't like the look of that hole.

Golden Retriever

This adorably goofy creature has often headed the most popular dog breed lists in many countries, and it's easy to see why. First, its beauty—with its soft, pale yellow coat, expressive gaze, and gaily waving tail, there are few other breeds that match it in the looks department. Add to that its hardworking nature, sweet temper, unwavering loyalty, and puppyish playfulness, and how could anyone resist? The golden retriever was first bred to retrieve ducks and other fowl for hunters, but is now more in demand as an all-round family favorite.

Life expectancy 10–12 years | **Height** 21–24 in (53–61 cm) | **Trainability** Eager to learn and smart | **Grooming** Daily brushing and frequent baths | **Exercise** Lots, as they are prone to putting on weight | **Likely to say** Give me a job! | **Unlikely to say** I'm in a bad mood.

French Bulldog

Every dog has its day, as the saying goes, and the days of this little charmer have arrived: in 2018 it overtook the Labrador retriever as Britain's favorite breed, and did the same in the US in 2022. Despite its name, the French bulldog originated in Nottingham, England, whose lacemakers emigrated to France, taking their little companion dogs with them. With its large batlike ears and appealing expression, this canine clown will steal your heart.

Life expectancy 10–12 years| **Height** 11–13 in (28–33 cm) | **Trainability** Easy if you make it fun | **Grooming** Occasional brushing | **Exercise** Two fifteen-minute walks a day and lots of playtime | **Likely to say** Take me please! | **Unlikely to say** Let's go on an eight-mile hike!

Barbet

The barbet is one of the breeds developed to retrieve shot birds from water, and its webbed feet enabled it to move easily across the canals and rivers of France, where it got the nickname "mud dog." The barbet's proper name, however, comes from the French *barbe*, meaning "beard." If you look at its handsome face, it really does have a beard! An old breed, the barbet has been recorded as far back as 1387. It is related to the poodle and the briard, and may have played a part in their breeding. It has a fun-loving nature, making a delightful family pet.

....

Life expectancy 12–14 years | **Height** 19–25 in (48–64 cm) | **Trainability** Intelligent | **Grooming** Daily brushing | **Exercise** Loves to retrieve, so play catch as well as taking walks | **Likely to say** It's the perfect day for a swim. | **Unlikely to say** That water looks chilly.

Coton de Tuléar

It might look like a child's toy, but this is a little creature with a big nickname—the Royal Dog of Madagascar. The coton de Tuléar is thought to have existed on the island for centuries and is named after the Madagascan city of Tuléar (now known as Toliara). The word *coton* refers to its soft, cotton-like coat, a distinctive feature of the breed. And its personality is every bit as appealing as its looks. The coton gets along with just about everybody and is pretty low-maintenance—as happy in a large house as a small apartment. Its clownish antics and happy nature have won many hearts around the globe.

Life expectancy 15–19 years | **Height** 9–11 in (20–28 cm) | **Trainability** A quick learner but needs firm handling | **Grooming** Brushing a few times a week | **Exercise** Not much but hates being left alone | **Likely to say** I love everybody! | **Unlikely to say** I hate everybody.

Rhodesian Ridgeback

A line of hair growing backward along its spine gives this handsome scent-hound its name. The ridgeback comes from what is now Zimbabwe, where it was used by hunters to track lions, bears, and wild boar. The breed originated by crossing European dogs with those of the Indigenous people of southern Africa, whose dogs possessed this same ridge of hair. A pronounced ridge was thought to be a sign of courage. That may be unfounded, but the Ridgeback is certainly brave and more frequently used these days as a guard dog because it is so protective. Though energetic, it will happily snuggle on the sofa with you after a decent walk.

Life expectancy 10–12 years | **Height** 24–27 in (61–69 cm) | **Trainability** An intelligent dog | **Grooming** Weekly brushing | **Exercise** Decent daily walks | **Likely to say** I will protect you. | **Unlikely to say** Eek! Spider!

Index

About the Author

A former newspaper journalist, Nicola Jane Swinney started writing books about horses and, everyone knows, where you find horses, you will also find dogs. Having been around horses and dogs—mostly hunting hounds and gundogs—for most of her life, it was almost inevitable that she would end up writing about them. She now has cats in the shape of two Maine coons and a husband who is far down the pecking order. She says if she were a dog, she would be a golden retriever: blonde, always somewhat disheveled, a bit goofy, and far too interested in food!

About the Illustrator

Romy Blümel is a German illustrator based in Berlin. Her work looks as though it has been linocut, but in fact she works with paint. She draws directly on the surface of paint, as well as drawing in ink, and combines the two mediums to create the beautiful artwork you see in this book. Her work has been featured by a broad list of clients for newspapers, magazines, books, advertising, and cultural events.